The Best Seat in the House

Tim Noel

Parson's Porch & Company

The Best Seat in the House

Parson's Porch Books

The Best Seat in the House

ISBN: Softcover 978-0692358917

Copyright © 2014 by Tim Noel

All rights reserved. No part of this book may be reproduced or transmitted in any form or by any means, electronic or mechanical, including photocopying, recording, or by any information storage and retrieval system, without permission in writing from the publisher.

To order additional copies of this book, contact:

Parson's Porch Books
1-423-310-8815
www.parsonsporch.com

Parson's Porch Books is an imprint of Parson's Porch & Company (PP&C) in Cleveland, Tennessee. PP&C is an innovative non-profit organization which raises money by publishing books of noted authors, representing all genres. All donations from contributors and profits from publishing are shared with the poor.

Table of Contents

Wealth and Poverty	7
How to Mismanage a Miracle	11
Passing through the Gate	16
Parable of the Pounds	21
The Sower	26
The Mustard Seed	30
When God Visits	34
One Lost Sheep	38
The Lost Boy	42
The Poetry of Hope	46
Two Men Praying	49
The Good Samaritan	54
The Best Seat in the House	60
The One Who Turned Back	65
Redeeming Thanksgiving	70
For All the Saints	74
Something about Mary	78
Before Evangelism	81
Fairy Tales	85
Crossing the Line	89
Bread of Heaven	93
The New Normal	98
Faithful Thomas	102

Wealth and Poverty
Luke 14:25-33

Jesus taught the disciples, "None of you can become my disciple if you do not give up all your possessions."

I have this Yellow Lab named Dessie, who has recently developed an attachment to me, follows me everywhere I go. Stalking, is what it is. If I stand still, she does, too, just looks at me. If I sit down she lies down at me feet. My family thinks it's adorable; I think it's driving me crazy. I sometimes wonder if Jesus felt that way about the disciples.

You may have read about Zen for smart alecks: Do not lead me for I may not follow; Do not follow me for I may not lead. Basically, just leave me alone. I wonder if that's how Jesus was feeling when he talked to the disciples about following him.

When I was a teenage I knew what it meant to follow Jesus. We all went to a camp up in Michigan, Camp Bambi. The campfires, worship services, singing "I have decided to follow Jesus," all this had a profound effect on my. "No turning back, no turning back." It was about that time in my life that God called me to ministry, and I've been following ever since.

It is a harsh passage in Luke! But if you look at the context in Luke, Jesus is halfway through his journey up to

Jerusalem. Luke dedicates ten chapters to telling the story of that journey.

In this passage, Jesus said to the disciples, "Follow me. Go with me up to Jerusalem. Stay with me." This following would not be easy for any of them, no "there and back again" experience. They wouldn't be staying at the Holiday Inn, nor was there a *per diem* for their meals. They would leave family behind. This journey required full commitment; but follow him they did, all the way to Jerusalem.

Well, for us today, it is not the same. No cross ahead, no arrests likely. So, can we just skip this whole "follow me" part? Probably not.

The reality is, the claims of Jesus for our lives are still daunting, even today. Jesus is claiming priority in our lives! As much as we love our houses, Jesus comes first. As much as we are dedicated to our family, Jesus bids us accept him as Lord, and to offer it all up.

The offer from Jesus is no casual venture, putting your name on the roll of the church and dropping some money in the offering plate. This commitment is major, one of the biggest things we'll do in our lives.

So what if we say, "No"? What if we go instead for Door Number Three? Well, guess what? God will not punish us! No lightning bolts, no fire from heaven, no punishment. We still get to be Christians, still beloved, still Presbyterian. But, our lives will be diminished, I think. What we miss out on is the journey with Christ.

You see, even though the demand is great, the rewards are beyond measure. Jesus invites us to be in relationship with

God through him. Follow him, and we'll find ourselves walking with Christ along the way.

We will witness lives being transformed, changed to be more like Christ. And we will get to know Jesus more intimately, to learn of him.

Paul described it as the difference between living merely at the level of tangibility, living in the "flesh," on the one hand, and living in the spirit on the other. And it's not, if we opt for a spiritual life, that we give up the things of the flesh; but that they become balanced in Christ. They take their proper perspective.

When human activity is out of balance, even good things can sour. Sexual relations, given by God for procreation and for expression of love, can become manipulative and violent. The worship of God can degenerate and become less about worship of God and more about idolatry. Even friendship and family, which can bring us such delight, can be places of strife, anger, and jealousy.

But Paul says that when we live in the Spirit, walking with Jesus, the Spirit brings love, joy, peace, patience, kindness, goodness, faithfulness, gentleness, self-control. This is what our journey with Christ brings us. The more we are in his company, the more like him we become.

As we walk with Christ with fidelity, our perspective on ourselves and the world will change. We will be more patient with ourselves, and others. We will be more able to sort out the issues of our lives. We will find ourselves loving enemies, forgiving sinners, praising God, laughing with friends, and being at peace with ourselves.

When we are discouraged in our lives, when we are weary, we find strength from the one who walks with us.

The other word for this journey is salvation. Salvation is not a transaction that we make with God, but a pilgrimage that lasts a lifetime. Time and time again Paul says that we are saved by faith in God, but a better translation is that we are saved by God's faith in us. We go off to a far country, but God still believes in us. We wander off and pursue the prizes and baubles of life as if they were God, but God is faithful to us.

We follow God in the most circuitous route, but God is steadfast and true. Even when we go through the valley of the shadow, we don't have to be afraid, because God is with us.

The decision to be a real disciple of Christ is too important to be made by the lake, by the fire, late at night while the camp leader makes her pitch. Truly, a person could sell anything to anybody at Camp Bambi. No, what we are deciding involves our very lives, and should be discussed and decided in the light of day with our best resources at our disposal.

How to Mismanage a Miracle
Luke 12:13-21

If you have children, you have heard the complaints, usually voiced right after you laid down the law. "No, you can't go to the party." Or, "That's right, you have to be home by 10:00." "I don't care if your friends are all driving Porsches, you cannot have a Mercedes!" You know what is coming next, and so you brace yourself for it. "Dad, that's not fair!" "Tell Sally to stop bothering the cat; it's my turn." "Mom, make him share his stuff with me." "But I want it!" "I hate you; you're the worst Dad in the world!"

Listen to a story. Once there were two men whose father had died. The first son, being the elder, had two thirds of the estate coming to him, and the younger brother, one third. That was the law, and whether you were the firstborn son or the second, it did not matter. It might not seem fair, especially to the younger son, but it is the way it is.

The Father had died, and so it fell to the older brother to handle the estate, pay the outstanding debts, and divide up the estate between himself and his whiny little brother. But much to the dismay of the younger son, his older brother was taking his sweet old time dividing it up.

Frustrated, the younger brother came to Jesus and said, "Make my brother share with me!"

He came to Jesus. Stop and think about that for a moment. Jesus was wandering around the countryside, teaching new and outrageous ideas. Besides all that, he evidently was healing the sick, giving sight to the blind, and maybe even raising the dead.

The younger son came to Jesus, and all he wanted to talk about was his inheritance, trying to enlist Jesus to intercede on his behalf. This young man did not need Jesus, he needed small claims court.

If you could stroll up to Jesus this morning, face to face, what would you say? What would you ask? What would you do? I mean, would you really ask him for a stock market tip? Perhaps you might say, "So, Jesus, how do you like the football team this year? I think we might make some noise in the league!" This man comes to the Savior, the Son of God, and the best he can do is gripe about money!

Surely we would not do something like that! On the other hand, maybe we would. It is not that different than us, though, is it? We come to church preoccupied with sports, finances, family. Even when we say our prayers, usually we ask for something for ourselves, a few dollars more, perhaps. Does it ever enter our minds that we might begin with praise and adoration? In this time, in this place, is there anything more important than praise? But too often we are too busy for that.

So, in response to the younger son, Jesus told a story. The land of a rich man brought forth plentifully. Evidently that was nothing new; the man was already rich.

No one was expecting such bounty. He said to himself, "Where am I going to put all this stuff?" Certainly this kind of harvest would never fit in the barns he already had. So the rich man decided to pull down his barns and build bigger ones. Once the harvest was socked away, the man could retire early, play golf, maybe buy a new car.

It is a nice story with a happy ending, don't you think? Except it was not the end. God came to him that very night! "You fool," God said! It is powerful and even disturbing language! But God continued, "This night your soul is required of you; now who gets the stuff?"

The farmer did nothing wrong. In an occupation like farming, where all kinds of things that can go wrong, this time everything went right; it was amazing. So what is wrong with this picture? Why did God find fault?

Jesus said to the young man: Beware of every form of greed — the word really is covetousness! It is one of the 10 Commandments, but we don't make a big deal about it. This is one of the commandments that a person can break, even repeatedly, and not get in trouble. You will never read the headline: "Minister resigns church in shame! She had coveted her neighbor's car!"

It makes you wonder why covetousness is included in the Ten Commandments! Yet there it sits, alongside stealing, lying, and murder.

What is covetousness, anyway? Covetousness means desiring to have what belongs to another. But it is more than just a sly look at his riding mower in the garage. Covetousness is accumulating more and more stuff, beyond what a person really needs, and still wanting more.

Look again at the parable Jesus taught. The bumper crop in the parable was about the same as winning the lottery; and not one of those little twenty million dollar payoffs, split four ways, but a really big one. So the farmer said to himself: What can I do with all this food?
Well, look around you! This parable takes place in the Gospel of Luke. In other words, the farmer lived in a world populated by beggars, and cripples, the destitute, the down

and out. People literally starving to death, but the rich farmer keeps it all for himself.

No wonder God says, You fool! The farmer is a fool to think that life is money. He is a fool to think he can live to himself, and die to himself. He is a fool to think he has no responsibility to God or neighbor.

We are not given to know how the younger brother reacted to the teaching of Jesus. He came to Jesus about the inheritance. He wanted only what was his, what he had coming to him according to the law. But something in him made Jesus think of this story about covetousness, with all its dangers.

The response of Jesus would remind the younger brother (and us!) that life is not about how much you can get! For that matter, the lesson is really not about money at all. It is about what we want and what we need. The parable of Jesus is about where we look to find happiness, meaning, and joy in life. For some people happiness is indeed about money; but it can be about sex, or power, or status. But do any of those things offer more than a fleeting amusement?

We do live in a world of great wealth, side by side with unimaginable poverty. This parable is never more applicable than it is for us today. We who live in the United States casually consume the lion's share of what our world has to offer, and we should at least be aware of that.

We also live in a world where some people of wealth have come to realize that great wealth comes with a great obligation. These are people who give half of their fortune away, or even as much as 95 per cent, to help the needy.

We so like our stories in this country. We like rags to riches, tales of underdogs who come out of top. But what does all that mean?

Jesus did not come to earth to make us feel guilty about money. He came to set us free. Free from the power of the world. There is indeed a miracle in the story for today. It is not the miracle of gaining great wealth. No. The miracle of the story, the miracle of our lives, is coming face to face with Jesus. We all receive so many expressions of God's love every day. We get up in the morning. We feel the chill in the air, or the warmth of the sun on our faces. We say hello to our family and friends. If we are lucky, we come to church.

The true bounty of God is the love of God. God's love is enough for the younger son, and the elder son. It is enough for you and me and all the people in the world. It is enough for us and for our enemies.

This bountiful love has come to us, full and free. And you would think that we might open our hearts and our purses so that our neighbors might have enough to eat. Just out of love. Amen

Passing through the Gate
Luke 16:19-31

The gospel of Luke tells the parable for today, about a rich man and a poor man who lived side by side. The rich man feasted sumptuously every day and wore the finest clothes. The poor man, named Lazarus, was hungry most of the time, and the dogs licked his sores. Both men died, which is the one thing they had in common, and in Luke's upside-down world, the rich man went to the place of torment while Lazarus went to paradise.

That story was common in Jewish lore in the days of Jesus. It was told to console people who were always on the bad side of town, people whose lives never worked out. The story gave hope, that even the poorest of people can find an eternal reward; even the rich, who always seem to get away with murder, will come to judgment.

But in Luke's version, the story does not end there. Instead, the death scene becomes a springboard for conversation between the rich man and Abraham. The rich man complains, "Father Abraham, I'm thirsty. Could send Lazarus to get me some water?" This rich man in his time has had people who would fetch and carry for him; so why should it be any different now?

But Abraham replies, "No! The days when the poor might fetch for you are over. While he was at your gate you did nothing for him; now it's too late. Pay back is indeed a no fun."

The rich man, undeterred, moved on to his second concern. "Well then, could you at least send Lazarus back to my brothers," says the rich man. "They have lived just like I have, so it makes sense they might end up in the same place. But, I don't want them to come to this place of torment."

Abraham replied: "They have Moses and the prophets – let them read their Bibles!"

The rich man said, "I know they have their Bibles! We have all kinds of Bibles! It looks good to have a few lying around for when visitors come around. But none of us actually read it! I mean, have you actually tried to read the Bible? It is difficult to understand, and never seems to tell me what I really want to know. But if someone came back from the dead, they would believe!"

"No," says Abraham, "if they don't listen to the Bible, neither would they believe if someone should rise from the dead!" And the story ends right there.

I can understand the consternation of the rich man, can't you? Abraham seemed to be very laid back when it came to evangelism, didn't he? Basically he said, just put the Bible out there in the general vicinity. People will read it, and it will do its work.

But the rich man wants more than that! He wants a revival service with the evangelist preaching, the kind you hear in a tent in August when the heat feels like eternity has come and it's not working out as we'd hoped.

This was his family he was talking about, and he desperately wanted them to end up in a better place than he had. After all, you can't just educate people, or hope they'll read the Bible! But a dramatic, gut wrenching sermon with a long invitation will do the trick. Or better yet, a miracle would work well. Have Lazarus come back from the dead and they would believe!

A good friend of mine found himself at church on a Sunday night when he was nine years old. The minister began to preach about fornication. People who do this, he said, will go to hell. My friend had no idea what fornication was, but he looked around at all the blue haired women who were in church that night, and he figured, whatever fornication was, chances are none of them had done it. So the preacher must have been talking about him. Scared half to death; my friend walked the aisle, repented of his fornication, and was gloriously saved.

But Abraham said, Let them read their Bibles. If they don't believe the Bible, neither would they believe if someone rose from the dead. Now, if Abraham was right, it suggests that the results of our ministry do not depend on the volume of the sermons, or the eloquence of the minister. The style of worship and whether there is an altar call are unimportant.

Luke's theology is that the Word stirs people, moves them, and generates faith! And faith cannot sit still while people suffer.

My friends, if you live in the pages of this book – really live in them, not just use them for sermon ideas or to prop up your personal theology – then you will not be able to eat a full meal in full view of a starving person, and do nothing about it.

So why did the rich man wind up in a place of torment? Was it because he was rich? Of course not, any more than Lazarus rested with Abraham because he was poor.

We really know next to nothing about the rich man, but we do know this: Whatever faith he may have claimed, it never led him through the gate to help poor Lazarus. The faith that can sit back and take it easy while people starve is not real faith; because real faith transforms us.

What that means for us is, we must find expression for our faith, and the way to do that is to reach out to those who are hurting. We respond to the needs of the world in whatever ways we can – with our hands, and heart, with voices to read to children at elementary school, by visiting people in the prison, feeding the hungry, and caring for the elderly. We will pass through the gate, paying attention to those who are hurting before our very eyes.

There is a legend in Jewish tradition about a man named Lazarus. He was a servant of Abraham. Genesis 15:2 tells about him; his Jewish name was Eliezer. According to the legend, Abraham sent Lazarus back to walk the earth. He was to report back to Abraham about how Abraham's children were doing – did they observe the Torah? Did they treat the poor well? Did they show hospitality to strangers?

Maybe that's what the story of Lazarus that Jesus told is all about. Lazarus, sent to earth once again to keep up with the children of Abraham. Lazarus, sitting there at the gate of the rich man, covered with sores and starving to death. Finally going back to Abraham with his report.

And what if he returned today? What if he lived among us? Are we doing all that we can, or does poor Lazarus sit and hope for scraps from our tables?

Of course, Lazarus does not dwell among us. But keep in mind that Jesus taught, "Whatever you have done, or left undone, to the very least of those around you, you have done it unto me."

So let us all pass through whatever gates might stand between us and those in need, and bind up their wounds, and feed them, for Christ's sake. Amen.

Parable of the Pounds
Luke 19:11-27

In some ways it is like going on a vacation. There are so many things that need to be done before we even get in the car. We have to take the dogs to the dog hotel, and the cats to whatever palace meets their standards. We tell the neighbors to keep an eye on the house, and hope they won't break into the house themselves. If we're lucky, we pawn the kids on some friends. We leave what matters most in the care of those we trust.

That's kind of what God did – created this world then turned it over to humans, allowing us the authority, freedom and creativity to take care of things for a while. Creation, someone said, was the moment when God ceased to be everything so we humans could be something.

Which brings us to the parable for today. A man went on a journey, and entrusted his property to his three servants. He gave those five talents, two, and one, respectively. A talent – this has nothing to do with tap dancing – is how they used to measure money; one talent was about as much money you could make at McDonalds in fifteen years.

The first two servants took the money and invested it in the stock market. The third man was afraid, so he took the money and hid it in the ground – not even a passbook savings account.

The master of the estate returned from the trip. Each of the first two servants had doubled their money (obviously a very bullish market). The master said, "Well done, faithful servants."

Then the master came to the third servant, who said, "Master, I knew you were a hard man, reaping where you did not sow and gathering where you did not winnow, so I was afraid. I went out and hid your talent in the ground. Here it is."

The first two servants become models for us. Their attitude about life is refreshing. They show us something of what it means to be made in God's image – in the image of a creative and dynamic God. We are situated in a universe that is full of mystery; it does not always seem to be fair or faithful. But God wants us, even in the face of life's uncertainty, to live life fully and joyfully.

C. S. Lewis used to tell his students that there are two ways to approach life. They could choose the way of manipulation, to finagle their way to quick power, taking the shortcut to influence without developing the skills necessary for that responsibility. Or they could choose the way of discipline, to learn thoroughly and well, to become good workers, which is how we are faithful in this world.

The parable seems to teach that God cares what we do with what we are given. God does not expect us to be another Moses, or Abraham, or Mother Theresa. God wants us to be ourselves, our best selves, to do the best with what we have.

These first two servants lived whole-heartedly. They were willing to risk it all. But this third guy played it safe. He was given money and did nothing with it. He had only one talent to begin with, and may have been afraid to lose it.

When I was in the eighth grade I was on the school basketball team, despite a lack of height. Or shooting ability. Or anything. I was the sub who sat on the bench behind the best player on the team. I entered the game, if I did at all, when we were way ahead and it did not matter. Even then, although the game was virtually over, when the ball came to me I passed the ball. I knew I wasn't very good, so I never took a shot.

I guess maybe many of us play small roles in the drama of life. But we should, nonetheless, play them well and with enthusiasm. If I had it to do over, I would have jacked up a few shots just for the fun of it. Maybe one would have gone in.

The third servant sinned by what he left undone. A sin of commission might have been wasting the money on wine, women, gambling. But his sin was cold unfaithfulness, the sin of doing nothing. It's what Paul talked about in Romans, "falling short of the glory of God."

He was afraid.

Fred Craddock tells a story from his adolescence:

> A pretty girl moved into our town and into our school. She was immediately popular. Admiring her from a distance, I asked her, in the privacy of my mind, to go with me to the movies. I looked at her, then I looked at myself; and, in the privacy of my mind, she said no. For days afterward I was both hurt and angry at her rejection of me, a decision she was never allowed to make.

The third servant was afraid, and we've been there – afraid to ask someone for a date, afraid to voice our opinions, afraid even of God. Well, you can understand why, given the way most people seem to think about God.

Zephaniah said, "The great day of the Lord is near, near and hastening fast; the sound of the day of the Lord is bitter. That day will be a day of distress and anguish, a day of ruin and devastation, a day of darkness and gloom."
And 1 Thessalonians teaches, "When they say peace and security then sudden destruction will come upon them."

I grew up with that kind of preaching, and it can mess a little kid up for a long time. Lightening and thunderbolts, warnings and commandments can all be a little daunting. But when it came time for God to speak a Word to us that would let us know God better, what God spoke was Jesus. Just when you decided God was about law, obligation and punishment, Jesus came along and invited us to freedom, joy and serendipity. God sent Jesus into the world so that we might have life, full and free. Good life.

God wants us to live our lives fully, not out of fear. Sometimes that means taking a risk, rolling the dice.

Did you hear the words the master spoke to the first two servants, who lived with zest? "Enter into the joy of the master." That's what God wants for us.

There is a Taize chant that says it well:

> In the Lord I'll be ever thankful,
> In the Lord I will rejoice.
> Look to God; do not be afraid;
> Lift up your voices, the Lord is near.
> Lift up your voices, the Lord is near.

If you find yourself these days between faith and fear, there is a better way. God has given all this to us. Now enjoy it, let go a little, and live joyfully in the image of your God. Amen.

The Sower
Luke 8:1-8

In three of the four gospels, the teachings of Jesus often took the form of parables. A parable is a story that reveals God's activity in the world; and because it's a story, it can be interpreted over and over again. So maybe we might hear a new word today, one we haven't heard before.

The parable of the sower tells about a man who goes out with a pouch across his shoulder, filled with seeds; and he begins to sling the seeds across the field, covering every corner, hoping for a good crop. Jesus explained the parable for the disciples. The seed, he said, was the word of God. Well, I used to think that this was a story of evangelism – we spread the word hoping that some will accept it and be saved.

But surely the parable is more than about evangelism. The word does not come to us only for our initial conversion; rather it comes to us, for our salvation, every day of our lives, if we would only listen. So the parable of the sower is a parable for every day of our lives; the question is, will we receive it?

Some seed fell on the path, and the birds ate it up. In Israel, fields might have paths through the middle, packed down and hard from the people who walked them. Because of the hardness of the path, the seed could not sink down into the soil but sat on top, where birds could eat it.

It is a picture of our lives, so busy. We wear it like a badge of honor! If you aren't busy, you are doing it wrong! We spend our time running from one thing to another, and taking the time to read the Bible and meditate on it, well, it is not going to happen. The word is there, proclaimed in church, or waiting to be read in the Bibles we have laying around the house, unopened.

Other seed fell on rocky ground. In Israel in the days of Jesus, rocky ground was about all they had. The shallow earth received the seed and it sprang up quickly; but when the sun came out, beating down on the plants, they withered away because their roots were insufficient.

Receiving the word requires a depth of soil for the plant to be able to take good root and survive. I remember when my wife's grandfather died. Becky was given his Bible, and she look to see which passages he had underlined, and what comments he had made. But the comments revealed a simple, shallow understanding of faith, and she was disappointed. There is nothing wrong with a simple faith, but over the years we are expected to learn more, receive the word more deeply into our hearts, and have a mature, meaningful faith.

Some seed fell among the thorns, which choked the seed. Jesus told the disciples that the thorns were the concerns we all have, the things that wake us up in the middle of the night. Or the longing to be rich; the desire for more stuff.

These things – cars and I-phones and golf clubs – are not bad in and of themselves; but spend too much time chasing after them and, well, our priorities can get messed up.

Some seed fell among good soil, and yielded a bountiful crop. I think we all have all these tendencies within us, including the ability to be the good soil that is so useful. In your life, be the good soil, and receive the Word.

I think all four of these images describe us – too busy, or not enough roots, or choked by thorns. But there is good soil there as well, don't you think?

When I was at seminary I also served as pastor of a small church in Western Kentucky. I enjoyed my time there, doing what I do, and the church treated me very well.

I had not been there too many months, however, when a member of the church asked if I would make a hospital visit at the Veterans Hospital in Louisville, to a man who was not a Christian; in fact, he was considered to be the town sinner. Well, it was a small town, and there was not much competition.

Come to find out that every pastor who came along was asked to visit with this rascal, and time and again he sent them packing. So, I braced myself and went to see this old sinner and introduced myself; eventually he told me that a young chaplain had been visiting with him and he enjoyed their conversations; and I was glad. Sometime later I went to visit the man again, and he told me that he had become a Christian through the ministry of this chaplain.

When the patient died sometime later, it fell on me to do the funeral service. I told about the young chaplain and that the man had become a Christian.

Weeks went by, and I was asked to visit one of our homebound members, a matriarch of the church. Eventually she said, "I heard that in the funeral service of this person, you said he had become a Christian!"

"Yes," I replied, "that is what he told me."

The woman puffed herself up and said, "Well I want you to know, that if he can be a Christian, anyone can!" I think she said that to put me in my place; but I heard it as the gospel of Jesus Christ.

Thanks be to God. Amen.

The Mustard Seed
Luke 13:18-19

Being the age that I am, I have a memory from elementary school. I don't know if this still happens today, but I hope it does. Every now and then we would walk into Mrs. Stewart's fourth grade class and see the shades drawn and a movie projector set up. Folks, this was release for the captives. The movie projector meant no studying, no learning, not having to go to the blackboard to reveal how much you do not know. A movie meant no questions to be answered, and no mathematics. It probably also meant that the teacher had had enough of us for a while, and needed the movie as much as we did.

Sometimes if the teacher was feeling really good, she would run the movie in reverse. And we would laugh at people running backwards, people who had fallen being jerked to their feet, buildings that had been demolished coming back together. We were laughing, I suspect, at life being undone.

The parable of the mustard seed is one of several parables about seeds in the Bible. The parable of the sower, with his bag of seed slung over his shoulder, casting the seed almost haphazardly across the ground, waiting to see how it would all turn out.

The seed growing secretly, a kind of parable for city dwellers: the man plants the seed and then goes about his business, and after a while life springs forth and the Sower has no clue how it all works.

The parable of the Mustard seed revolves around the size of the seed as opposed to the size of the plant that grows from the seed. It's a small seed, but when you plant it, it produces a tree, well, actually more of a shrub; but the shrub would be big enough for birds to rest on its branches.

There are two ways to interpret this story. One is to view it as a parable of growth. You plant such a small seed, but something substantial comes for the little thing.

When I played softball as a teenager we had one real slugger on the team. He always hit the ball a proverbial country mile. Except one time: instead of a towering homerun he hit a screaming line drive at the third baseman; the poor kid did not have time even to get his glove up, the ball hit him in the center of his chest and knocked him back about ten feet. The batter would have been safe at first if he had bothered to run, but he just turned and went to the bench. We were shocked, and asked him, Why didn't you run? He answered, The ball didn't go far enough.

If the parable of the mustard seed is a growth parable then it would say to us that the Kingdom of God is more about infield singles and hustle than steroid powered homeruns.

But I have come to believe that this story is less about growth, more about miracle.

In Jesus' day the Hebrews would see the seed and see the plant, side by side, and rather than thinking about the process of growth they would think about the miracle of new life. Place them side-by-side, the seed and the plant, and you can't get from the seed to the plant, not without a miracle.

Jesus taught that life happens when a seed falls to the ground and dies. That's how this story would speak to us.

It is a story about the places in our lives where we have experienced death, and how abundant life springs forth from that death.

This story invites us to re-examine the situations in life that are hopeless. What loss are you experiencing today? What fear or pain darkens your days? It might be the death of one you love, or the death of a dream. Maybe your career has gone south on you, and you no idea how to go forward. Perhaps a relationship that has made your life what it is has come to an end. Whatever it is, no matter how hopeless it seems, nothing is beyond the power of God to redeem. God is still at work. God is still God.

This does not mean that everything will necessarily work out as we would wish. I remember recently passing a young woman in the stairwell at the hospital in Danville. I heard her weeping into her phone, telling the news that was breaking her heart. Things don't always work out as we want.

But God still works, not only in the events but in our hearts. Sometimes the miracle is not what occurs physically but what occurs spiritually; not so much that there is healing, but that God gives abundant grace to bear the burden; and who is to say which is the greater miracle?

The parable invites Easter to work its way into our imagination. If the Mustard Seed is about growth, we need to be optimistic. But if it is an Easter story, it demands more than optimism: it calls for faith. Because in this kind of story, in this kind of world, we are not the Sower – God is. And what comes forth from the seed is beyond our power to produce.

Isn't that what this parable is all about? That one day long ago the Sower sowed a seed. It fell to the earth and died;

but out of that death came life, and all of the little ones are blessed by that life. And in response we become resurrection people, believing that God never gives up on us, and that death is not the last word.

My daughter and I went to see the last Harry Potter movie this past week, and don't want to give anything away for you; you are going, right? Towards the end one of the main characters dies, and the little boy two seats down from me began to cry. I wanted to tell him to not give up on the story! This movie is set in the world of magic, and in that kind of world not even death has the last word.

We do not offer – Jesus never promised – a life free from pain. But Paul promises us, "In all things God works for good." In the midst of every desperate situation God is at work; and Jesus offers himself, and the hope that sometimes we find the movie running in reverse: resurrection from addiction, and new life from deadly past.

And we come to understand that life is not a problem to be solved but a gift to be lived by God's power and God's love. Amen.

When God Visits
Luke 7:11-17

We hear today from Luke the message of God's presence in our lives. Luke refers to these moments of God's presence as a visitation, a special time in our lives when we sense the presence of God more keenly than at other times.

At the very beginning of Luke's gospel, before the birth of Jesus, Zachariah proclaimed to Mary,

> *Blessed be the Lord God of Israel, for He has visited and redeemed his people (1:68).*

Here, in Luke 7, when Jesus raised from the dead the only son of a widow, the people said,

> *A great prophet has arisen among us!*
> *God has visited his people!*

Finally, at the end of the gospel, just before the crucifixion of Jesus, he wept over Jerusalem:

> *Would that even today you knew the things that make for peace! ...but you did not know the time of your visitation.*

Obviously this theme, of God's visitation, is important in Luke. God visits us. Sometimes it is translated, God understand us, knows the joys and the fears of our lives.

It is a vivid expression of the presence of God in this world. God has visited.

In a sense, of course, God is always with us. Paul wrote to the Romans: You don't have to go up to heaven to bring Christ down, or to the abyss to bring Christ up; Christ is near you, on your lips and in your heart. Jesus is Immanuel, God with us, and we are never alone.

Sometimes the presence of God's is very evident. Certainly when Jesus was born if was a time of God's visitation; but at the birth of every child God is present, God visits us. One of the most mystical times of my life was when my daughter was born. After the birthing, when all the cleaning up and foot printing, and weighing were over, she was handed to us, mother and daughter and father; she was so solemn and quiet, as if she knew that this was important, staring at us. God visited us that day.

In the story from Luke 7, Jesus visited a widow at Nain at the death of a son. It was a time of great sorrow – a woman who has lost her husband, and now her only son. God through Christ visited her, and rescued her.

And we wonder if at any death, any crisis, God is near.

You've seen the photo shop picture of the twin towers burning on 9/11. Smoke billows up, and in the smoke you see the face of the devil. But if evil is present at such a horrific event, surely God also draws near.

The trouble is, sometimes we miss it, miss the visitation of God. Anything happen today? Well, the Queen dropped by, but you were out.

Luke tells a wonderful story about the risen Christ drawing near to the disciples on the very day of the resurrection.

Two disciples were leaving town, headed for Emmaus, when a stranger joined them. They talked about all that had happened that day; the one they thought was the Messiah, but the rulers had taken him by force and crucified him. They told this stranger that the women had claimed that Jesus was risen from the grave.

But even while they were telling the story of Jesus, they did not recognize Jesus. God has drawn near, but they didn't know it until he broke the bread, and in that act Jesus was revealed to them. The Son of God dropped by, and they didn't know it.

How tragic for us, not being aware of God. But it happens all the time. Carl Sandburg: The doctor drops by the pub and someone asks if anything special had happened. The doctor said, No. Mrs. Lincoln just gave birth to a baby boy. For some people a birth is just another baby, and a death is no big deal. They live their lives as if God does not exist, practical atheists.

No wonder when Jesus came to Jerusalem, when he saw the city Luke says he wept over it.

> *Jerusalem, Jerusalem, Would that even today you knew the things that make for peace! But now they are hid from your eyes....because you did not know the time of your visitation.*

How tragic it is, how horrible to think that Jesus walked this earth, God with us, and people did not know him. He came to redeem us, to give us new life; he brought with him all that we would need for peace, and we just shrugged.

So, what are we to do? At the very least, we should live in the moment and be aware, so that we might catch a glimpse of the mystery of our lives. On the golf course, I try to look around at the beauty of God's creation; it is usually the best thing that happens when I play golf. I try to see the face of God in the faces of my friends, listening for God in their laughter.

We are called to a different kind of life, to be aware of the presence of God with us every moment of every day. In moments of silence and meditation; or in times of prayer; we might develop an ability to find God in others – all of us created in God's image. It is a way of living that might change our lives; and in that change we might find peace and joy.

For the widow at Nain, Jesus did not just give her back her son; he gave her back her life.

I try not to judge the theology of others, because I surely do not have all the answers. But I did see a comic strip, B.C., by Johnny Hart. All the guys were lined up carrying signs: The first sign read, "Jesus is coming again in ten seconds." And so the signs counted down the mystery: nine, eight, seven…

But the coming of God into our worlds, our lives, is not so limited, is it? Jesus visits us every day. He never really left. Amen.

One Lost Sheep
Luke 15:1-10

In the book and movie, *The Legend of Bagger Vance*, Rannolph Junah was a young man with the world by the tail. The Savannah native was born with rare ability as a golfer and married the daughter of a millionaire. But World War 1 came along, and Junah signed up to lead young men into battle.

So one night, with shells exploding and bullets flying, he gave the order for his men to charge the enemy. Junah and his men charged out of the trench; barbed wire all around, bullets and chemical weapons. Soon Junah was the only one standing, and he could not go on. He quit, quit the war, quit his marriage; just walked away from his life. He was lost, don't you think? He had lost himself.

In the text for today, Jesus told a story for people who are lost. What man of you, he said, if you had a hundred sheep and one because lost, wouldn't leave the 99 out in the wilderness and search for the one that was lost? Jesus asked the question in such a way, you could tell he wanted you to answer, "Why, sure, I'd do that!" But I wonder.

You are familiar, perhaps, with the old gospel hymn that Tennessee Ernie Ford sang, *The Ninety and Nine*.

> There were ninety and nine that safely lay

> In the shelter of the fold;
> But one was out on the hills away,
> Far off from the gates of gold.

But that's not how the story goes, is it? The 99 sheep were not safe in the shelter of the fold; they were out in the wilderness, totally vulnerable to any wild animal that might come upon them!

What Jesus was really asking: "Wouldn't any of you who had 100 sheep, if one of them went astray, leave the 99 out in the wilderness and set out to find the one lost sheep?" The answer, of course, is "No!"

No one would take such a risk. You do that, you end up getting fleeced!

The name of that story would be, "The Parable of the Idiot with one sheep."

Now, the same parable is told in *The Gospel of Thomas*. You may not know this gospel – it did not make it into the bible. But the story of the lost sheep is different in *Thomas*: The sheep that wandered off was the largest, most valuable of the flock; it was state fare, blue ribbon sheep. It could probably talk….

Now the story begins to make a little sense. You might risk all the other sheep, the scrawny ones, for this special sheep. But in Luke, it's just a sheep. It was not the smartest sheep, nor the cutest. I was an ordinary sheep.

You may have seen *Antique Roadshow* on PBS. People haul stuff from their garage or attic, lug it down the studio for the experts to see, hoping that something in their life has value. The expert always wants to know, "How much did you pay for this?" The woman with the junk wants to know,

"What is it worth?" "I paid $46 for it five years ago." "It's a Picasso, and it's worth millions."

This is what we want, but Jesus is not giving it to us. The little lamb gets saved, but it is not worth much.

So, how do we make sense of this parable? The only way the story of the lost sheep makes any kind of sense is if we take our proper place in it. We are the lost sheep. Come to find out, the lost sheep can be educated and live in nice homes. They feel lost and lonely, guilty and ashamed. They are you and I, at one time or another in our lives.

In this story, we don't get to be the Shepherd, saving the day. We are not even one of the 99 good sheep who have sense enough not to get into trouble. No, we are the one that gets itself lost, because we are perfectly capable of ruining our lives. Ah, now it makes sense!

The activity of the shepherd is still folly; but now it dawns on us that it is the folly of grace. We hope against hope that the Shepherd will play the fool one more time, risking everything to rescue us. Because that is our only hope.

That, of course, is what God did. God through Christ gave up all that God had; God launched out into the wilderness to find us; and when God found us, God picked us up and brought us home, rejoicing.

In the story of Bagger Vance, Bagger is the caddie who came to Rannolph Junah to help him find his authentic swing, his true self. The story has its twists and turns, times when you think Junah is going to get his life together, turn it all around, and other times when you think that nothing can save this poor man. In other words, it is the story of your life, and mine.

Finally, when you think things cannot get any worse for Junah, they do.

He finds himself way off the fairway, deep in the forest; and faintly he hears the bombs and bullets from his earlier failure. He reaches to pick up his golf ball, ready to give up on the game and on himself, to quit one more time. But Bagger would not let him quit on himself.

I guess we all get ourselves into places like this – why, even churches get lost from time to time! But the Shepherd comes to us, and bids us to continue. We find a way forward. And once we have been found, the Shepherd sends us right back out to help the other lost sheep find their way back home. Amen.

The Lost Boy
Luke 15:11b-32; 2 Corinthians 5:16-21

Well, Jesus was misbehaving, again. He was out there with sinners, shady characters, and people of ill repute, laughing and having fun. Everyone with any sense knew, in those days, as they know now, that the old adages were true. You really are judged by the company you keep.

The Pharisees, those paragons of virtue, were watching and saying, "This man receives sinners and eats with them!"

Jesus did not answer them directly, was not all "in their face!" Instead he unleashed on them not one, not two, but three of his parables. There was a man who had 100 sheep, and when one was lost he left the 99 to fend for themselves while he searched out the one lost sheep. There was a woman who had ten coins, so she lit up all the candles and did a sweep of the house, searching for the one that was lost. And there was a man who had two sons.

We call the third parable The Prodigal Son, although Jesus never named it. It really is more about the Father than either one of the sons, a Father who loved his sons even though they were a mess.

Just look at them. The younger son came to his father one day and asked if he could receive his share of the inheritance right now. In other words, "Dad, I don't want to wait around until you die. Can we pretend you are dead so I can get the money *now*, not have to wait until you die?"

Believe it or not, the Father agreed, and soon after the young son headed out to the big city. The bible calls it a far country; I'm thinking it was New York City. But the actual location does not matter. I guess in one way or another we've all gone off to that country before. In your marriage, it's when you find yourself staring at the TV, reading the paper, and ignoring your spouse. We all know about the far country.

Sooner rather than later, the money ran out and this lost boy began to be in want. The only job he could find was feeding pigs, and he was so hungry that the Purina Pig Chow was beginning to look pretty good to him. This is a subtle sign that you have hit bottom.

Down there in the pig pens, the younger son came to himself. There are people, of course, who are skeptical about the genuineness of the son's awakening, but who can judge the mystery of the human heart.

The language, though, is the language of grace: the son came to himself.

He repented of his sins: "I've sinned before heaven and against you." And he turned back home, towards the Father.

The son was not expecting much – just make me one of your servants… But the Father received him, well, as a son! The father ran to meet his son. He gave the son a robe, which was a garment of honor. The ring the father gave was a sign of authority. The sandals were a symbol of freedom. And threw him a party.

About the time the party really got rocking, the elder son came in from the fields and knew something was very wrong. He heard the music, and he knew that Dad never listened to music. The older son looked and saw that a party was in full swing; Dad was putting on a feast. Finally he realized the reason for the party – his lousy little brother was back home. And he was furious.

This older brother was, in so many ways, such a good man, keeping all the rules, slaving for his father. And the unfairness of the situation was evident for all to see. The father throws a party for the younger son who wasted all that he had received from the father; but the father never gave a party for the older son. It was not fair!

But his Father said, Everything I have is yours, son, but we absolutely have to throw a party. Your brother was dead, and is alive. We have him back.

What a good father – a good man with two lousy sons. The younger son wasted all the money and preferred the party life to family life. The older boy kept all the rules, but his bitterness and moral outrage kept him from loving his brother.

You see what Jesus has done? The Pharisees, who were righteous, loyal, but unforgiving, complained about the party Jesus attended for a whole room full of younger sons and daughters. They were sinners.

But in the story Jesus told there were two different kinds of sinners, and a Father who loved them both. He loved the younger son enough to allow his impertinence, to give him the inheritance early, and to receive him back home. He loved the elder child enough to go out to him, to assure him of his love, and to invite him inside.

You and I are in the mix somewhere. Sometimes we are that younger child, and sometimes the older child. But with or without us, this party is going to happen!

When I was a little boy I got in trouble one day at school. The teacher had announced that we were going to watch a movie, and I guess my excitement carried me away. So the teacher sent me out into the hall with these words: "You can come back inside and watch the movie when you've been out there long enough." So there I was, out in the hallway, listening to the movie and the laughter of my friends; I wanted so much to go in, but I couldn't figure out if I'd been out there long enough? It's hard to figure out when you're a little boy.

Eventually I went back into the classroom, and no one protested that I had not spent enough time out there in solitary confinement. But it was such a shame. I missed so much of the movie. Amen.

The Poetry of Hope
Luke 21:5-19

Two texts from the New Testament call us to the topic of the trials of the church and persecutions of the children of God. Historically for those early Christians, The persecutions occurred twice. Under Emperor Nero in the 60s, when the church was driven underground, and accused of burning Rome itself. And under Emperor Domition in the 90s, when the church was hounded, and some church members denied their faith.

The perspective of Luke's gospel is to look forward to the persecution that lay ahead; and Revelation looks back at the persecution that has already taken place, as a multitude of believers who endured it all stood before the throne of God.

What is interesting is that these are usually thought of as a sign of the absence of God. We even ask the question, when times of personal or corporate trial come to us, Where is God in all this?

But the Bible teaches just the opposite, that these times of pain and sorrow are signs of the presence of God.

- That nothing goes on in the universe that God does not know;
- That God has foreseen all of this;
- And that God is never nearer to God's children than when we are hurting.

You may have seen the photo-shopped picture of the smoke rising from the twin towers on nine eleven, and in the middle of the smoke is the shape of the devil.

- I'm not sure if the devil was there that day;
- I am sure that God was there, heart-broken like the rest of us, comforting and strengthening his children.

Jesus taught us that these things must take place!

- When all that is holy and lovely to you looks like it is going to be destroyed; but do not lose heart;
- By your endurance you will gain your souls.

This is what I want to talk to you about today. How do we endure in times of great grief? How do we have faith in God when our world is being destroyed?

If we think of faith as an individual matter, we might be in trouble. Times come for all of us when our faith is shaken by events. But we are not in this alone. Our faith is corporate. We are in covenant with God not just as individuals but as a body.

We endure as a body of believers. We believe and hold on as a group.

There is a time-honored saying in the Anglican Church, that schism is worse than heresy. Now, we believe just the opposite, don't we? That is all right to divide and destroy the church over orthodoxy; but the truth is, it is all right for us to disagree, even for us to be wrong, but it is not all right for us to let go of one another.

The real challenge of the church is not whether we can always get our doctrine correct – I mean, get real! No, it is whether we can, as Paul put it, work out the implications of our salvation by loving each other. And that means, not just getting along with the sweet, gentle church members who would not hurt a fly; no, it means staying in relationship with the rest of us!

Staying in touch with one another, holding onto each other through all the stormy blasts – this is how we know God is still with us.

- Come earthquakes, famines, plagues, scary stuff in the skies…
- We are to hold onto one another – we are to endure – because holding onto one another is how we hold onto God!

Barbara Brown Taylor told the story of a group of young women decided to climb Mt. Washington one day. They climbed up the mountain and watched the sunset, but they did not count the cost. By the time they headed down the mountain it was getting late, and a heavy fog was creeping in. Soon they could not see a thing, not even the person in front of them.

The women decided that they would hold hands and not let go, no matter what. And so they began to make their way down the mountain, halting and faltering, stopping to discuss what they should do and which way they should go. Finally they made it to the bottom of the mountain, worn and frazzled. They were only able to find their way because they refused to let go of one another.

That is what God has promised us – "Lo, I am with you always." And that is how we should hold onto each other." Amen.

Two Men Praying
Luke 18:9-14

Across the street from the last church I served was a Speedway, which I'm sure has suffered now that I've taken my business elsewhere. It's not so much the gas I put into my car, but the junk food I put into my body. One day I was leaving the store with my Diet Coke and Little Debbies when a young man began to talk to me. He had seen my badge from the hospital, which identified me as a chaplain. So I confessed that I was a minister. He wanted to know where I went to church, and I nodded at the Presbyterian Church, and he was not impressed. He told me that being a minister was not going to get me to heaven; and I was thinking, okay, but it won't automatically send me to hell, either. He was one of those religious types who thought they were the only ones going to heaven. So we spent a while talking past each other:

- I am a Christian.
- No you're not.
- Am too.
- Are not.

I guess those conversations are just the chance you've got to take if you want to live in the Bible belt. And come to find out, it happened in Jesus' day, too.

Two men went up to pray, a Pharisee and a publican.

We know a little about the Pharisee, or at least we think we do. We tend to dismiss them as hypocrites; but there is more to them than that. The Pharisees were the most religious people in all of Israel in the days of Jesus. Their very name means "pure." They were pure in all things –

- They observed the Law;
- They were very patriotic;
- They avoided all contact with the impure.

So when the Pharisee in the parable stood and prayed, he was probably being very sincere.

- He fasted twice a week, more than would be expected.
- He tithed of all that he owned.
- And the Pharisee was thankful he was not as others.
    - Thieves, rogues, adulterers…
    - "Case in point," he thought, looking around at the publican. "I sure am glad I'm not like that guy!"

A publican was a tax collector. Tax collectors were at the very opposite end of the social spectrum.

- No occupation was more despised or looked down upon.
- Whenever a country was conquered, the Romans recruited opportunistic individuals to collect taxes.

    - Charge more than is due, and keep a bunch for yourself.
    - Pay some to your boss, and there is no problem.

- Tax collectors were getting rich on the backs of their fellow citizens.

Both of these men came up to the Temple to pray.

- The Pharisee prayed about his morality; there was no confession, no repentance, and no need for forgiveness.
- The tax collector could not even lift up his eyes, but beat his breast and prayed, "God, be merciful to me, a sinner."

Then Jesus, in a judgment that would have stunned his listeners, pronounced that the tax collector went away justified rather than the Pharisee.

Who is the good man here? By any objective standard, it is the Pharisee. So why does the tax collector go down forgiven rather than the Pharisee?

Maybe it's because he never asked for forgiveness. He saw no need to be forgiven. He was already righteous.

Beyond that, since when does religion have to be competitive?

- It's not enough that I am right – you must be wrong!
- Not enough that I have faith – you must not have any!
- I am righteous – which means you must be a sinner. I wonder why we do that.

We turn the story of God's grace into a rat race, in which we must excel, we must do better than others, and we must come in first.

Why do we do that? I suspect it's because we really don't like ourselves or accept ourselves; therefore we cannot accept other people.

- What would happen, I wonder, if we really came to understand that God accepts us?
- Maybe we could accept ourselves, and each other.
- And when that happens, then we find grace, for ourselves and for each other.

We can stop harping about our own righteousness. We can let God be the savior.

When I was a chaplain at the hospital, one day I was making my rounds. I was chatting with a woman who was about to have surgery, and I asked her if she'd like me to pray with her. So she asked me what church I was with, and I said, Presbyterian. And she declined my prayers. So I asked her about that. She said, "Well, I'm a member of the Holier than Thou Church, and we're the only ones who are going to heaven."

- I replied, "Surely you don't think I'm going to hell?"
- She replied, "I'm very sorry, but it's not me; it's what the Bible says."
  - Now, I checked it out, and I'm here to tell you that nowhere in the Bible does it say that Presbyterians are going to hell.

Well, I got even with the woman. I went out into the hallway and prayed for her.

As I read the Bible, none of us are righteous on our own, none of us good enough to get into heaven. What we need is a good dose of the grace of God.

A group of compassionate people, touched by the struggles of children who were physically handicapped, decided to have a festival for them. They promoted it and lots of physically challenged children attended. There was cake and ice cream, games and prizes, and everyone was laughing and having fun.

One of the adults saw a little boy who was standing outside the large room, staring longingly at all the kids having fun. The grown up went out and asked the boy, "Why don't you come on in?" And the little boy replied, "I can't. There's nothing wrong with me." Amen.

The Good Samaritan
Luke 10:25-37

Let's play, dress up in costumes and see if we can get into character. The script for today is Jesus' story which we commonly refer to as "The Good Samaritan."

Which part do you want? Why not try them all and see if they fit.

Traveler: He was walking the path from Jerusalem down to Jericho.

- There is something reckless about him, because everyone knows it is not the kind of road a person should be travelling! Those who explain away the tragedies that happen all around us would have a field day on this one.
- You know what happens to this person, of course. The story is legendary, so well-known that even those who don't care much for the Bible and its stories know what happens in this one.

    o Accosted by thieves, beaten and stripped bare like a car parked in the wrong part of town.
    o Left there in the ditch, too wounded to help himself, looking so dead that everyone who comes along must deal with the possibility that to touch him would be touching a corpse, which would render the passerby ceremonially unclean.

- Left for dead. Recently I heard that the mother of a friend of mine had died. It doesn't really matter how I came across this information, because this kind of information in a small town is both quick and accurate. So I sent a nice note of consolation and talked about how much I liked her mother, which I did. Only, it turned out that she was not dead. Awkward.
  - Appearing to be dead does cut down the chances of receiving aid.

- Putting yourself into this role would require some imagination, or a good memory. Most of us have reached a place in our lives that looks very much like a death. Do you remember? How did it feel not to be able to choose your helper?
  - How badly are you hurt? Are you bleeding?

The next role in this drama is that of the thieves: They plied their trade in the hills near the road, waiting for the vulnerable to come by.

- In that regard, they are not that different than any number of organizations in our society.

  - Health care is sometimes a competitive venture. Without going to the trouble of digging up statistics, doesn't it make sense that rich people are healthier, live longer, and are treated with better regard than the derelict who stumbles into the ER on a Saturday night late. The vulnerable.

- Finances. It is hard to invest in retirement when you have nothing to invest. When you have to choose whether to pay the electric bill, or the rent, or buy food for the family, you probably are not checking how your 401K is doing.
  - Politics. Money buys a person access and influence with the elected officials; poverty not so much. Oh, the occasional drive through the slums and government housing make a good photo op for the politician, not to mention how these people either deserve our help because they are needy or that they do not deserve our help because it would only make them more dependent on the government.

- None of us, surely, would ever behave like the thieves. But I do remember driving towards an appointment with a fellow minister. It was a narrow road and traffic was bad. I barely got a glimpse of the car on the side of the road, the people standing by it, the obvious need. The story of the Good Samaritan flashed briefly through my mind as I continued on my way. The appointment was important, and the time was tight. I mentioned the car beside the road and how it made me think of the Good Samaritan, two religious types barreling along on the other side of the road. My friend suggested we go back; I resented him for it.
  - We don't want to get into a discussion of what drove these people to a life of crime! It complicates the role too much, complicated our lives too much, to find a motive, a reason, for what they did. Better

just to assume that they were simply thieves because they were too lazy to work.

The third group in this drama consists of the priest and then the Levite, and they are supposed to be the good guys. After all, they are in the business of being good guys; so why aren't they?

- What could possibly be so important that it kept them from stopping to help?
- Were they hesitant because they did not want to get their hands dirty? Sometimes the story of the person in the ditch is so good that it makes a riveting homily illustration, which in itself is a very good thing! In fact, it is better to convince others to stop and do the right thing when they see the need than it is to stop oneself. Morality in this instance is so slippery.
- How to play such a role? Are we to act holy and self-righteous, assured that the person who was left in this state must have been a sinner, or this would not have happened to him! After all, it did not happen to me! Hard to argue with that kind of reasoning!
- Were the priest and Levite at all uncomfortable with this situation?

The best role in the story, of course, is the Samaritan himself. Imagine being so well known for this one act of kindness that the Samaritan is never referred to merely as the Samaritan, but always the Good Samaritan!

- Of course, if we do our research into this role we would find that Samaritans were not considered by the Jews of Jesus' day to be good at all. In fact, they were assumed to be rather bad. They were hated. They had an uncanny knack for getting it wrong:

Wrong politics, wrong religion, and wrong ethnicity!

-
  - Every now and then you'll hear a story about some person who stopped and helped, did the right thing, and they are called a Good Samaritan. If the woman who helped out is at all humble, or even has a sense of what is expected, she will demure.
  - "Oh, don't call me a *Good* Samaritan; just a Samaritan will do!" Having no idea, no clue at all, that the words "good" and "Samaritan" don't go together at all, are in fact a real early example of an oxymoron!
    - "Just call me a Samaritan," call me outcast, call me unclean, call me the one you'd cross the street if you saw me coming, so heinous am I.

Once we've come to realize who the Samaritan is, we might have to rethink what it means to be the one in the ditch! He must have been nearly dead, or else he would have told the Samaritan not to bother, that he had already called Triple A, who would be along at any moment. How desperate this poor person must have been!

The story, of course, always makes us think of Jesus. Jesus is the One who came to us when we were just about dead. Jesus treated our wounds, and carried us to a place where we'd be okay. Jesus picked up the tab for our healing.

The fact is, we can put ourselves in any number of roles in this story. At times we have been traveling along and gotten ourselves in a horrible fix, and needed help. At times we've been too ready to prey on the vulnerable, to cut them off, to treat them badly. We have been too religious to do what we should do, like the priests and Levites. And every now and then, we behave like the Samaritan did. We act the way Jesus would have.

And when we take that role, we are following Jesus Christ. Amen.

The Best Seat in the House
Luke 14:1, 7-14

It's really more like playing musical chairs; as soon as the music stops, someone is going to left without a seat, and usually it's a little guy like me. That is what happens when even a dinner party becomes a competition.

Take the wedding banquet that is described in the gospel lesson for today. It would have been the event of the year for any small village, and everyone would have been there. And, of course, Jesus was there, standing off to the side, taking it all in.

Jesus watched all the invited guests scrambling to get the very best seat in the house, and after a while he announced that they had it all wrong. Instead of the best seats, we should be seeking the worst seats.

Well, that doesn't make sense! We spend most of our lives figuring out how to get ahead. Make yourself presentable, make some money, connect with the right people, and join the right clubs. Then when it comes time for the big event of the year, you get to sit at the head table! That's how it works. Life is one big competition! The one who has the most toys when he or she dies…wins!

Then Jesus comes along: If you're invited to a fancy dinner, do not take the best seat in the house, no matter how superior you might be feeling.

- Because, what if Prince William shows up, or Justin Bieber, and how embarrassing would that be?
- You'd have to give up your really good seats for them, and by then all but the lousy seats would be taken, you know, right by the door to the kitchen.

What's more, Jesus said that if you are throwing your own soiree, do not invite the people who are wealthy, who'll be throwing their own party and they'll return the favor. Instead, invite folks who are not on the A list, or B list.

- Invite the bums, the drop-outs, the down-and-outs.

This is a strange mathematics; but it is the very heart of Luke's message. Luke is about radical reversal. The mighty will be pulled down, and the lowly will be elevated. The last will be first, and the first will be last.

When I heard this message as a little kid – okay, I was a nerd, I admit this – I figured out my strategy for life. If the last shall be first, we need to work very hard to be last, so that in the end when the last shall be first, tada, there we are!!!! We get to be first when it really counts. You cannot kid a kidder, my friends.

Except, maybe that's not what it's all about – not about making the poor rich and the rich poor. All that happens when you do that is you get a change in who's on first, like the move "Trading Places." Maybe it's about leveling the playing field, so that everyone gets something, and no one is out in the cold.

Think about that for a moment. We are Presbyterians! We believe in grace. The Christian life is not about status, contrary to what I learned in my youth.

- We sang, Will there be any stars in my crown?

- o I wanted stars in my crown, not just some plain gold thing!

- Preachers would proclaim that some would be "Saved, but by fire."

  - o You get to heaven, but you smell like hell.

Is that really what it's about? Is that what our faith comes down to?

The banquet is at God's table. None of us could afford the tickets in our wildest dreams. But – and here is the punch line – it is free. Free for you, free for me, free for the poorest of the poor.

Years ago I had a dream. I dreamed that I had gone to heaven. Evidently I had died, but that part was not in my dream.

- Heaven was shaped like a giant cone.
- People were placed on each level according to the amount of good stuff they had done.
  - o Go to church, that is level one.
  - o Read your Bible, level two.
  - o Give to the church, that is, like, level 20.

In my dream I realized that at the very top of this mountain would be God, and I wanted more than anything to see God.

- I began to climb.
- But when I got to the top and pulled myself up to the very peak of heaven, it was not God. It was the devil.

- o This was not a happy ending to the dream.
- o I woke up deeply troubled, literally shaking.

I have had a long time to unpack that dream. Any religious system that places people in the very best seats of heaven based on how much good they do on earth…God is not at the top of that system. It is the devil.

We do indeed believe in grace. That is how we are saved, and that is the basis of our relationship with our Father.

- We do not earn it by our goodness.
- We are given it by a loving God.

  - o Turns out that none of us are on the A List!
  - o We are all pretty much the same, the Bible says.

    - We all sinned.
    - And all our good deeds? Paul says they are like last year's fashions. No good.

"When we all get to heaven," we'll all be welcome, all be loved, and all will rejoice in God.

Does that mean it does not matter whether we do good things on earth? Of course not! But it's not about how we live, but **why** we live as we do.

- If you think that living well will make God love you and let you into heaven, you've got it all wrong!
- But if you know that God loves you, and want to please God with your life out of gratitude to God, you are not far from the Kingdom of Heaven.

The invitation has already been sent out. None other than the Son of God carried it to this earth. And as evidence of how much God wants us at the party, Jesus lived for us and died for us. Whatever you do, don't miss out on this one. It really is the event of your life! Amen.

The One Who Turned Back
Luke 17:11-19

What is the greatest need in your life right now? If you had asked the ten people who came to Jesus that day between Galilee and Samaria, standing there at a distance because they were so highly infectious, they undoubtedly would have answered, "What kind of question is that? We need to be cured of this leprosy!"

The modern name for the disease is Hansen's disease, but whatever you call it, it is horrible.

- In Jesus' days, people with leprosy could not live among people, so they formed their own colonies.
    - They lived in cages, away from cities and towns;
    - Notice that even when they came to Jesus, they stood at a distance. No intimacy for these folks, no embrace; only fear.

- Lepers, of course, were not allowed anywhere near the Temple; so there would be no offering for their sins. There were cut off from God.
- There was no cure for leprosy, and it was usually fatal.

From the distance, they cried out to Jesus for mercy. It is a word that is used for alms, a bit of money tossed in their direction. They could not have imagined the amount of mercy they received.

Jesus addressed the need of their lives. He told them, "Go and present yourselves to the priest." So they went, and along the way they were cured of their disease.
But was that really their greatest need? No, the greatest need for men and women is to know God better than by hearsay. The spiritual life is an attempt to do something about it. That is what these men really needed.

One of them received it. He had an "Aha!" moment. He figured out something the others did not.

- It must have been something like, "Wait, I had the leprosy, then this guy named Jesus told us to go see a priest, and suddenly we were healed, clean as a new born baby."
    - They were all on their way to see the priest, where they would be pronounced clean and could start their lives over.
        - They would be respectable.
        - Maybe they would get a little apartment or even a house;
        - They would join "Matchmaker," find a nice woman.
- But this tenth man realized, "There is something more important than that! I need to worship, to praise the one who has healed me."
    - He realized that Jesus is the source of all blessings.
    - And as wonderful as the physical healing was, it was not what life was all about.

- o It all comes back to Jesus.
- o So this tenth man turned back, back to Jesus.

Many years ago there was a young minister, a delightful man who had a big life, loved to eat, loved sports. He was full of life and laughter, married and father of a beautiful child. But then he was diagnosed with cancer, a deadly cancer.

- His many friends visited him, sent him cards; mostly they prayed for him. They loved him, and they prayed for a miracle.
- But his cancer was not healed.
  - o It's hard sometimes, when you love someone deeply and pray with such intensity, but it does not seem to work.
  - o It raises all kinds of questions.
- The young wife, however, had a wisdom greater than her years. She knew that as wonderful as it would be for the cancer to be healed, there is something more important.
  - o The true miracle is not being cured of cancer, but of being sustained all your life by the love of God.
  - o And that's what her husband received.

In the story for today, all ten men were healed of their leprosy; but only one of them were saved.

What does it mean for our lives?

- We are tempted to think that all of our problems can be cured by getting more stuff.

- Thank goodness for the lottery, because it sustains our hope.
    - We can always win, even though we don't play; and all shall be well.

Now, I'm not going to kid you: I'd like to win it too.

- Money for a new car;
- Money for retirement;
- And maybe a better golf game.
- This is Janis Joplin religion:
    - "O Lord, won't you buy me a Mercedes Benz"

But in my best moments, I know better. All the money in the world would bring me only a temporary diversion. For real peace and joy, what I need is Jesus.

- If you want real happiness, and a satisfaction that is not dependent on your circumstances;
- If you want to see God all around you;
- If your life is not all you want it to be;
    - My goodness, only Jesus can fill those needs!

Look again at the tenth man:

- He turned back towards Jesus, which is the very definition of repentance.
- As he headed towards Jesus, everyone could hear him, because he was praising God with a really loud voice.
- He fell at the feet of Jesus, on his face in the dust.

- And he gave thanks.

That's pretty much where the story leaves us.

- The nine who were cured, I suppose, settled in and got jobs and raised a family. They became leaders of the community; they were prominent in the synagogue.
- But the man who turned back, I wonder about him. Jesus sent him on his way, it says. Jesus was not dismissing him, no, not at all. But Jesus was saying, your life has a different agenda now. You have received the gift of God's salvation; now it is up to live so that others might receive that gift as well.

Isn't that why we are here today? Amen.

Redeeming Thanksgiving
Luke 18:35-43

One of my favorite movies is the classic, *Shenandoah*. Jimmy Stewart played Charlie Anderson, a widowed farmer in the Shenandoah Valley in Virginia. Before she died, Charlie's wife had made him promise to raise their children right, to take them to church, and to say grace before meals. So he did, despite the fact that church and prayer did not exactly come naturally to him.

Still, he always said grace before a meal. He had one standard prayer:

> Lord, we cleared this land. We plowed it, sowed it, and harvest it. We cook the harvest. It wouldn't be here and we wouldn't be eating it if we hadn't done it all ourselves. We worked dog-bone hard for every crumb and morsel, but we thank you Lord just the same for the food we're about to eat, amen.

Charlie had never allowed any of his sons fight in the Civil War; but one day his youngest son, who was simply called Boy, was taken prisoner by soldiers. Charlie and his other sons set out to find him, and thus the story unfolded, a story of great pain and loss.

Finally, when the family gathered again at their farm, and Boy was still missing, somehow Charlie's standard prayer no longer worked. Charlie stammered and choked, but he could not pray.

The movie invites us to consider, What is the relationship between our circumstances and our willingness to offer our thanks to God? It is not an easy question for us.

- All of us can sing the hymn, *Now thank we all our God*, when the family is gathered safely and the harvest is bountiful;
- What do we do when peril is at the door?

Can we find it in our heart to celebrate Thanksgiving in hard times?

Today you heard a reading from Habakkuk:

> Though the fig tree do not blossom
> Nor the fruit be on the vines,
> The produce of the olive fail
> And the fields yield no food,
> The flock be cut off from the fold
> And there be no herd in the stalls,
> Yet will I rejoice in the Lord.
> I will joy in the God of my salvation.

Sometimes the fig trees do not blossom in our lives, and the flock is cut off from the fold. We are broken beyond measure, and the standard reason for this season falls so far short of our reality.

When that happens, we can either become bitter, or we can redeem our way of doing Thanksgiving. Rather than a "count your many blessings" Thanksgiving, maybe we can find it in our heart to express hope and confidence in the midst of our brokenness.

Habakkuk determines, "I will rejoice in the Lord, I will joy in the God of my salvation." And so we are reminded that

Thanksgiving begins not with our success or even with ourselves; it begins with God.

To be specific, the true meaning of Thanksgiving is that God gives us a second chance. God redeems us.

No one needs to tell you, no one needs to tell me, why we all need a second chance. As the prayer book puts it, we have not loved our neighbors as ourselves; we have failed in thought, word and deed. But the God of the second chance keeps loving and forgiving us. That is what Thanksgiving is about. It is God's forgiveness of our humanity, and our own forgiveness of each other.

The mercy of the second chance; after our failures and in spite of our flaws, God forgives. By the way, if you would like to redeem your Thanksgiving, you might do the godly thing, forgive the ancient grudge, and embrace the one who offends you. Don't do it for their sake, but for yours.

God's gift to us of a second chance means that we are not washed up, the book on us is not closed, and the last word has not been spoken or written in our lives. We have been, we are being, redeemed.

We are privileged to live, as W H Auden says, "for the time being:"

> Let us therefore be contrite but without anxiety…
> Let us acknowledge our defeat but without
> despair…
> [Because] the kingdom of heaven may come, not in
> our present
> And not in our future,
> but in the fullness of time.

In spite of our fumbles and because of God's grace

- we are not daunted by the troubles of this age,
- nor are we fearful of what is to come.
- We do not bless God for our wealth, our health, or for our feeble wisdom.
  - We bless God that God is, that we are, and that his promise and love shall be with us when time itself shall be no more. Amen.

For All the Saints
Luke 19:1-10

As you know, two days ago was All Saints Day, and the even before that was All Hallow Eve, or Halloween. We don't use the word "hallow" much these days, but it means to make holy. Abe Lincoln said of Gettysburg, We cannot "hallow" this ground, because the brave men who fought there have already done so.

All Saints Day is kind of an etcetera category, for the saints who don't have one whole day of their own, so we remember them today. But the lectionary did give us a strange story for today. You would think the reading would be about Peter, Paul, or Mary. Instead, we get this man who was not only a tax collector, but the chief tax collector. He was a sinner.

But, a saint is not a person of great righteousness, or even a person without sin! A saint is a sinner who has been redeemed. But if you pause to remember today those departed souls who have blessed your lives, we would do well to remember them as they were: They were people who were used in their lives to touch others, but they were also flawed, as we are. And in the end, all the praise for their lives should end up going to the One who redeems.

Everyone knew how Zacchaeus made his fortune, by cheating and betrayal. Human answers had failed for Zacchaeus, but that failure made him a candidate for grace. We are usually driven to salvation by failure. Life is not redeemed by the reasonable, moral efforts of men and women, but through the strange workings of grace.

The story captured my imagination when I was a little boy.

- So Zacchaeus climbed a tree to see Jesus; he was a short man. Wee little man.
- Jesus looked up, and salvation came down to a sinner;
- The Son of Man came to seek and save the lost.

Years ago that great Presbyterian minister, Maurice Boyd, told the story about meeting a new member of his family, a baby, at the airport. The baby was shy at first, not sure what to make of this new person who was getting into his personal space. More than one sweet child plays bashful when they meet someone new. Personally I tend to let it go, because they'll either come around or not, and I don't take it personally. But Maurice Boyd did not give up on this little tyke.

- So Boyd wagged a finger at him;
- He talked to him, and told him how handsome he was
- He smiled and paid attention without being too pushy.
-

After a while, the baby began to respond. He smiled at this nice man, and then laughed.

Now, whose faith was that? Was that the baby's faith, or Maurice Boyd's faith? Whose idea was it that the baby and Boyd should be friends?

Isn't that what God does with us? God takes initiative.

- God smiles us into smiling.
- God loves us into loving.
- God forgives us into forgiving.

That's what Jesus did with Zacchaeus! Jesus looked at him, called to him,

- "Zacchaeus, come on down! Because I'm going to stay at your house today!"

Well, Zacchaeus scampered down that tree. This man who was hated by all found love and acceptance that day. And the love of Christ in his life did its powerful work.

- "Half my goods I give to the poor!"
- "If I've cheated anyone, I'll make fourfold restitution!"

When Jesus dined that day with Zacchaeus, he was already on the outskirts of Jerusalem. He would draw near to the city and weep over it. He would come to the Temple and drive out the money changers. And everything would be set in motion.

- Jesus would take his place between sinners.
- He would find his own tree, and stretch out upon it, and give his live for all of us sinners who would be saints.
- And the world would never be the same.

God comes to where we are. We may not be sure about this One who has come, and maybe we even hide. But God will not be dissuaded, because we belong to him.

- God is patient with us, but He never gives up on us.
- And finally we give Him our hearts.

    o God smiles us into smiling.
    o God loves us into loving.
    o God forgives us into forgiving.
        - Today salvation has come to us;
          For the Son of man came to seek and save the lost.
          Thank God. Amen

Something about Mary
Matthew 1:18-25

Imagine with me what it must have been like for Mary. She was just a girl, really, about 14, betrothed to Joseph, but had not lived with him. As Matthew tells the story, Mary was found to be with child from the Holy Spirit. Matthew says nothing about an angel from God explaining anything to her about the nature of this conception. She must have been confused, and unsure of how things would work out. Meanwhile Joseph saw that Mary was with child, and he was inclined to divorce her quietly.

But God sent an angel, not to Mary, but to Joseph. The angel provided a different word, a different understanding of what was happening with Mary. The child did not mean the end of everything, but the beginning. What appeared at first to be a cause for condemnation, became instead a means of our salvation.

We don't know why Mary was chosen to bear this Child. The angel called her, "Favored one." God had chosen her, graced her, and singled her out to bear the holy child. Favored, indeed.

And Mary said yes. Of course, I found myself wondering if she was the first one to be asked by God. Maybe seven or 29 others… But Mary said yes, and she will always be honored and loved because she did.

Being favored by God must forever change the way she thought about herself. The Mother of the Son of God.

But while Mary is unique, she is not the only one who is favored by God. The story of the birth of Jesus tells us, more than anything else, that we too have been graced by God. And if we can really hear that, how can we not love ourselves? How can we not love each other?

I know that this is difficult for us to trust that God loves us – really, it's easier to trust God's love for other folks than for ourselves. We do not feel worthy. I wonder what it would take for us to believe God about who we are.

That grand Christmas carol reminds us:

> Long lay the world in sin and error pining,
> Till he appeared and the soul felt its worth.

That's what the story of Mary is about, Mary, the Favored One. That we are all favored. The appearance of Jesus is an expression of our worth, a demonstration of how much God loves you.

You know, the world is always telling us that we are worthless, and sometimes we let the world get away with it.

- You're not rich
- You are not smart
- You are not the right color, or ethnicity, or orientation
- You don't drive the right truck
- You're not very coordinated
- You are not pretty enough

But over and against everything the world said, we have the word of God:

- God created us, redeemed us, and loves us
- God through the infant Jesus appeared, and the soul felt its worth.

Mary was not worthy because of who **she** was, but because of who **God** is. And so we have great hope this year.

- A teenage girl is found to be with child 2000 years ago and her fiancé is thinking about getting rid of her, but God appeared and her soul felt its worth.
- A prostitute comes to Jesus…and her soul feels its worth.
- A man loses his job, and his family…but his soul feels its worth.

You don't have to believe what someone else says about you. No one else can determine your true worth, not even your pastor or you're your own self. Not even your parents or your children, or your church. **God has already made that judgment.**

- A child is born to you…and the soul feels it's worth
- Now will you believe that, and live? Amen.

Before Evangelism
Matthew 11:25-30

I first knew that God was calling me to ministry when I was 15 years old. Not long after, my father, who was my pastor, asked me to speak on a Sunday night. I focused on the Great Commission in Matthew: Go therefore and make disciples of all nations, baptizing them in the name of the Father, and of the Son, and of the Holy Spirit; and teaching them to obey everything that I have commanded you.

It was not until years later than I realized there is an earlier text that we have to learn before we can respond to Christ's Commission.

- Come to me, all you who are weary and carrying heavy burdens, and I will give you rest. Take my yoke upon you, and learn from me; for I am gentle and humble in heart, and you will find rest for your souls. For my yoke is easy, and my burden is light.

This is important:

- Before go into the world, we must come to Christ;
- Before we can teach all nations, we must learn from Jesus.

I hear this as an invitation to rethink evangelism. We need to find a way of revealing the very good news of our Savior so that it is consistent with who we are, and who Jesus is.

Listen to the language: Come to me… I will give you rest…

- Our little dog, Sasha, which evidently a Russian word that means "I will not!"
- One day Sasha managed to squeeze under the steps to our deck, a tight spot. She could not get out, so I came to her, speaking her name softly: "Come here, girl."
  - She replied, "I will not!"
- I said, "I mean you no harm; I only want to release you from what is trapping you. I'm here to help you, never to hurt you."

It is an invitation to grace, love, and mercy. It is about peace for our troubled souls, help in times of trouble, rest when we are weary.

- Come to me, he says. Learn of me…not just about me, but learn my ways, my heart.
  - Learn my love
  - Learn my forgiveness
  - Learn my gentleness
- Jesus says, "I am gentle, and humble in heart, and you will find rest for your soul."

I've told you before about efforts to convert me to Christ even though I was already a disciple of Christ. This has happened many times through the years; evidently I do not look like a Christian!

- But I understand these people! They believe that unless they convert me I will go to hell, so they pull out all the stops.

- But, of course, they cannot convert me, nor does my salvation depend on them.
- Only God can convert me.
- The best thing we can do is bear witness to the love of God. That's the best any of us can do.

So how do we bear witness to the love of God? Matthew's gospel gives us answers:

- "I was hungry, and you fed me."
- "I was thirsty, and you gave me a drink."
- "I was in prison, and you visited me."

God cares about people; God comes to us in time of need. Our lives ought to show people that we care for them.

I read about the evangelist who was out visiting during the week of the revival he was preaching. He came up to one person who told him that he was not a Christian. The evangelist talked to him about the life, death and resurrection of Jesus, but the man was not interested. He talked to him about heaven and hell, but he was not interested. He talked to him about the brevity of life, but he still refused. Finally the evangelist became angry and said, "Well then, you can just go to hell."

But, there was another minister who was out one night, and a prostitute walked by, a very young woman. The minister said, "God loves you." The woman walked on, then stopped and came back.

- She said to the minister, "Are you sure?"
- He said, "Yes."
- She asked, "Are you positive?" He answered, "Yes, I'm positive that God loves you, and so do I."

- And so they talked.

Now, which of those ministers do you think bears witness to the love of God? Yeah, I thought you'd know. Amen.

Fairy Tales
Matthew 13:44-52

Hearken back with me today to the fairy tales of your life. It might have been the Brothers Grimm, who gave the world *Rapunzel, Cinderella, Rumpelstiltskin,* and of course everyone's favorite, *The Mouse, The Bird, and the Sausage.* Or you may have preferred *Frankenstein and The Werewolf.* More recently we've had *Harry Potter.*

Fairy tales are important to us, and not just in childhood. All of us long for something out of that life, something more. We long for magic.

Well, hear the Word of the Lord! You listen to the stories from Matthew today and you feel like you have entered the world of fairy tale, a world where reason gives way to love and anything is possible.

It is a world where you see a "For Sale" sign on a tattered piece of property, and somehow you know there is buried treasure there. So you gladly give up everything to buy the property. Or, you find a pearl that is so beautiful that you sell the house, the car, cash out the college funds…and buy it.

That great preacher from the last century, Carlyle Marney, used to say that there is no agony in life more acute than those rare moments when you realize you paid too much. But sometimes, rarely, we find something of such worth that we should be willing to give up everything, to give our whole life, just to have it.; something of supreme value; something that comes along once in a lifetime.

Of course, we do live in the real world, don't we? After all, we are Presbyterians. It's hard to imagine our getting so carried away. What could possibly be so valuable that it makes perfect sense to turn our world upside down? Well, since we are in church and I am a minister, you probably think I'm going to say, "Only God is worth it," that life has meaning only when God is at the center of our lives, and that we would be wise indeed to give up everything else in order to have peace with God. And that is true.

But that is not what the stories of Jesus are saying. It is not that we find a treasure, and the treasure is God. Rather, God seeks and finds something of great value, a pearl of great price, and is willing to give anything, even himself, to have that treasure. And guess what? You and I are the treasure.

Now, that may not be how you view yourself. A lot of people go through life not liking themselves very much. We feel like we have failed at some level, that we are not good enough. We are frustrated with who we are. That frustration started early in our lives, and continues to this day.

Bernard of Clairvaux, a theologian from around 1600, wrote about the stages toward real fulfillment.

The first is **love of self for self's sake**. This is how we all start as infants. We are concerned about self, and self alone, which is as it should be at that age. We focus on our needs, and nothing else. Sadly, some people never outgrow this stage: It is always about them.

The second stage is **love of God for self's sake**. We have looked, somewhat, beyond ourselves in this stage, but we still try to have everything around us, even God, to serve our own needs. We want God because of what God can do for us. You can hear it in our prayers sometimes: "Give me this. Protect me from that. Give me the desires of my heart."

The third stage is the **love of God for God's sake**. This is when one senses that God should be worshiped and adored, not because of what God can do for us, but because of who God is. We delight, wonder, and rejoice in God.

This sounds like real spiritual maturity, but there is one more stage – the **love of self for God's sake**. Because in this stage we finally come to agree with God about ourselves, acknowledging that God knows us fully and loves us freely. We are able to say, I am created by God, redeemed by Jesus Christ, and I have been baptized into the Church. I am a person of worth.

Real spirituality leads all of us to say Yes. Yes to God. Yes to creation. Yes to ourselves.

- In creation, every day God looked at what God had done and said, That is good.
- But when God created a man and a woman, he said, That is very good.
-

If only we could agree with God. That is what Jesus was teaching: That we have value.

Here is the Kingdom of God: That God seeks us and finds us, and values us so much that God gives up the only Son to win us.

My friends, you are accepted. If we could believe that, we would have so much more peace.

Now, if you paid attention to the reading of Matthew, you might be wondering where that whole "gnashing of teeth" thing fits in. Matthew is big on weeping, wailing, and gnashing.

- What he is saying is, This is important!
- Because there are people in the world who have never entered the story of God's love. Their fairy tale is more like *Frankenstein* than *Cinderella*.
-
  - For these people, every day is about weeping.
  - They are living in their own hell, right here on earth.

I don't know what you believe about judgment, but I have come to believe that when we come to stand before God, it will be less like police court and more like a flower show; less concerned with punishment and more concerned with being shown how much we are loved. Because the One who judges us is also the One who loves us.

In God's eyes we are all a pearl of great price, a hidden treasure! Who are we to disagree? Amen.

Crossing the Line
Matthew 15:21-28

The story from Matthew for today is one that – well, if you were the minister, would you want to talk about this story?

- A woman came to Jesus seeking healing for her daughter.
- And Jesus was harsh, and downright rude to her.
    - His first response to her plea was silence, the kind of stony silence that conveys contempt.
    - Then he made it clear that she was not the right kind to be talking to him, that he came only for his own people.
    - Finally he compared her to a dog, which was the rather ugly word that Jewish people used to describe Gentiles, or non-Jews.
- Well, it is the assigned story for today, so here goes.

She was a Canaanite woman – which means not Jewish. She was from the wrong side of the tracks.

- The Canaanites worshiped different gods…
- They ate different food…
- They did not look or dress like the Jews.

No one was happy when she came to Jesus.

Not even Jesus! Earlier Jesus told his disciples to stay away from Gentiles. He said his ministry was only for the lost sheep of Israel. **Jesus had drawn a line, as clearly as if he had drawn it in the sand.** He said, **"Our ministry is to the Jews only."** After all, a person can only do so much. There are so many needy people, and we cannot help everybody.

You may know the feeling. We are here for the city of London, and the county of Laurel. Maybe some folks from Corbin. But really, these other folks have their own churches. We are doing our part.

But sometimes we come face to face with a person who does not look like us, or talk like us. They stand before us, this "other" person, one of "them" instead of one of "us."

This Canaanite woman was "one of them."

- She asked for help for her daughter – "Jesus, Son of David…"
- But Jesus would not say a word.
- The disciples chimed in, "Jesus, send her away."
- Jesus said, "You know, I'm only here to help my own people."
- She knelt and asked again asked for help.
- Jesus said, Should I take bread for the children and give it **to dogs**?
    - This is Jesus we're talking about here!
- Not to be put off, she replied, "You are right! But even dogs get the crumbs from the table!"
- And what could Jesus do? Her defiant refusal to take no for an answer, he called faith. And Jesus changed his mind.

At that very moment Jesus learned a lesson; a light came on in his head.

It was a pivotal moment in the ministry of Jesus. He had already defined his ministry – it was for his own people! But here is this woman, needy and insistent, and Jesus decided that **the line he had drawn might have to be erased.**

- Something in the woman cried to him;
- And something in Jesus melted. "Great is your faith," he said, and he gave her what she needed.

I guess we all draw a line somewhere in our lives.

- When I was a young boy, people did not know whether **cancer** might be contagious. And a lot of good Christians drew a line, out of fear, about ministry to people with cancer.
- **AIDS** came along, and we did not know how AIDS was contracted. I remember visiting people who had AIDS in the hospital, feeling more than a little trepidation.

Time after time in my ministry all kinds of people who are unacceptable have been placed before me. I think God has been trying to teach me something! I have visited people in the hospital and held their hands, and prayed with them.

At a church where I was Interim Pastor, one of our church members, David, a young man with AIDS, was well enough to attend church one Sunday. But during the service he became nauseous and went out to his car. After the service was over I grabbed a deacon and we went out to the parking lot and broke bread with David, and shared the cup there in his Pontiac; and I'll never forget it. Several months later I would say words over his coffin.

The lesson for all of us is that **the face of God** can show up anywhere. I remember one Sunday in Charlottesville when **a street person** showed up at the large, fastidious church where we attended. The street person walked into the sanctuary in the middle of the sermon and began to make his way down towards the front, crying out, "You don't care about me!" As he drew closer to the pulpit – and the elders began to wonder what they should do – the minister came down from that lofty pulpit and approached the man. The minister opened his arms and hugged him, saying, "I care about you! I care!"

From time to time we see the face of God in the strangest places. And we may be forced to reconsider an issue we thought had already been settled. When that happens, I hope we do the right thing.

- **May we be more hopeful than we have been before,**
- **More filled with grace,**
- **More open to the stranger who reaches out to the Christ who is within us.**

A friend of mine tells about three bedroom doors from his childhood – his, his brother's, and their little sister.

- Allen put a sign on his door – "Keep out!"
- Roger had a sign that read – "No girls allowed!"
- Little sister had a sign that said – "Everyone welcome!"

I wonder which room looked most like a church.

Amen.

Bread of Heaven
John 6:24-35; Ephesians 4:1-16; 2 Sam 11:26-13a

When I was a boy my mother would send me to the store to buy a loaf of bread; I don't know why she kept asking me, time after time, to go to the store for bread, rather than asking one of my sisters or my brother, because surely no one in our house could have been worse than I was at bringing home the bread. Oh, I would make it to the store, and would faithfully buy the bread. Without fail I would bring the bread home. But on the way home with that bread, it would be transformed into a football.

- And I would become Johnny Unitas or (Peyton Manning).
- I would take the snap and drop back for a pass.
- I would loft the ball downfield.
- Then, magically, I would be transformed into a wide receiver, racing down the field and catching the ball.
- I would tuck the ball under my arm and elude all tacklers until I made it to the end zone.

Every loaf of bread that I brought home was twisted, mangled, and squished.

My mother was a patient woman. Or maybe…her need to have an intact loaf of bread was not as great as her desire to see me happy.

The text for today is about bread. At the beginning of John 6, a large crowd had gathered to hear Jesus speak, and they had no food. So Jesus multiplied the few loaves of bread and fishes that a little boy had brought, and the multitudes were fed. It is a reminder to be hospitable, that when people are hungry we should feed them, real bread for hungry people; and when we have done it for the very least of God's children, we have done it for Christ.

You don't need me to tell you that; one of the things I love about this church is our commitment to the people around us as well as the people around the world. We need to be serious about that ministry.

But this is the Gospel of John, nothing is ever what it seems.

- Light and darkness, water and bread, all mean something more.
- Light:
  o Jesus is the one who lightens every person who comes into the world; He is the light, and the darkness cannot overcome him.
- And darkness:

  o When Nicodemus comes to Jesus it is night, and that tells us something about the darkness, the confusion of his life.
  o When Judas goes to betray Jesus, he goes into the darkness.

So it is with bread. After feeding the 5,000, Jesus teaches us that as good as it is to provide food for the hungry, pizza or cumquats, it is not enough. The trouble with food is that no matter how good the meal, hunger keeps coming back.

So Jesus uses the feeding of the multitude as a springboard for further dialog. He begins to talk about bread of heaven. By juxtaposing the bread that feeds the masses and this spiritual bread, Jesus is calling us to a different way of looking at the world, and ourselves, and each other. He is reminding us that life is more than biscuits! And if all the nourishment you provide for yourself is the bread of this world, you will not be a happy camper.

Now, I need to clarify: there is nothing wrong with bread; I eat bread, I have several friends who eat bread; I'd like my daughter to marry someone who eats bread. But what John's gospel is suggesting is that bread alone is not enough. Along with the food on our tables, we need to have a proper relationship with God, a vital spiritual life, which enables us to keep our material possessions, such as bread, in their proper place.

So when our spiritual life is what it ought to be:

- We will have a more balanced relationship with other people;
- And a proper understanding of what money is all about;
- And an ability to see God's work through creation;

The spiritual person does not have to give up food or sex or basketball; but in Christ all these things take their proper place.

Now, you need to know that I am not talking to you about an obligation, one more thing you have to do to be a good Presbyterian. No, I am talking about something that will fill the longing in your life.

- Have you ever found yourself staring into a fridge late at night?
- You're hungry, but you do not know what for.
-

Jesus speaks to that hunger, that longing, that emptiness.

What is the emptiness of your life trying to say to you?

For those of you who feel like life should be more; there is an empty place deep within you, and you've tried to fill it with pleasure, or money, or food; but nothing works. If that describes you, then hear the Word of the Lord: **There is bread available to you, and if you eat of this bread you'll have eternal life.**

- Eternal life: did you know that every time you see those words in the New Testament, it could be translated "abundant life."
- Jesus is not promising pie in the sky in the sweet by and bye; but real help for troubled lives in the midst of our days. Life can be more; yes, it can.

The food offered to us is spiritual bread, bread of heaven. I don't know where we got the idea that the things of the world, as nice as they might be, could ever give meaning to our lives! We are spiritual beings. "We are not human beings having a spiritual experience; we are spiritual beings having a human experience" (Pierre Teilhard de Chardin).

- We are spiritual; so let us live a spiritual life.

That hungering within us, that empty space that nothing else seems to be able to satisfy… That emptiness has the shape of God; what we are longing for is God. We are being called to God. And when we respond, over and over again on a deeper and deeper level, life begins to have meaning.

When I was working at Ephraim McDowell I would be called on to introduce myself to our new employees, a few sentences to let them know that I was a real person, just like them. So I would say that I had:

- Two dogs,
- Two cats,
- Two children.
- One wife; at a time.

Two cats. When our cats were quite small, it usually fell to me to take care of the morning feedings. I would go down to feed them in the morning before going to work, making sure that they had food and clean water; and I would always pet them. But one morning I was running late, so I rushed in and gave them their food and water and turned to leave. But when I looked back, they were not eating their food or drinking their water; they had climbed as high as they could on a chair, and were leaning as far as they could in my direction. More than they needed water, more than they needed food, they needed love.

Isn't that who we are? Climbing, leaning, yearning for the love of God. Amen.

The New Normal
Deut. 15:7-11; 2 Corinthians 8:1-9, 13-15;
Mark 5:22-24, 35b-43

Miracles play an important role in the story of Jesus in Mark's gospel. They say something about who Jesus is, the needs of the world, and reality. We all know about the needs of the world; they seem never to change. But Mark reminds us of another reality, that great power has come into the world, and that chaos no longer has the last word. Jesus bursts onto the scene in Mark, with no infancy narratives, no tender stories of angels and mangers and shepherds; he is just there, and he overturns the natural order of things.

Rabbi Joshua Heschel was asked what advice he would give to young people. He replied:

> I would say: Let them remember that there is meaning beyond absurdity. Let them be sure that every little deed counts, that every word has power, and that we can – everyone – do our share to redeem the world in spite of all absurdities and all frustrations and all disappointments. And above all, remember that the meaning of life is to build a life as if it were a work of art.

Every little deed counts, every word has power as we do our share to redeem the world.

And that brings us to the Gospel lesson for today.

- Last week…when we last saw our heroes they were in a boat on the lake when a heavy storm blew in. The waves were actually swamping the boat, and the disciples were scared half to death. You have to understand that the "lower lights" had not yet been invented. And Jesus was asleep in the back of the boat.
    - "Teacher, don't you care that we are perishing?"
    - Jesus says, "Peace, be still!" and the sea is at peace once more.
    - Jesus: "Why are you afraid? Have you still no faith?"

- Mark then tells the story of a man who was possessed by an unclean spirit. No one could control him, tame him. It's a word we use regarding animals, and it indicates that the towns' people thought of this man as less than human. Then Jesus showed up. He commanded the unclean spirit, "Come out of the man," and the man was restored to his right mind.
- Then comes the story appointed for today. Jesus crossed the lake and had not been on shore five minutes when one of the leaders of the synagogue, Jairus, fell at his feet. His little girl was close to death, and he begged Jesus to help. But before Jesus could follow him home, the worst possible news came. It was too late; she was gone. But Jesus ignored this version of the truth. Turning to Jairus, he delivered the shortest sermon of his career: "Do not fear, only believe."

    - And he raised her from the dead.

There's a theme at work in these stories. Jesus is the One who makes things as they should be:

- Restores calm to the sea;
- Restores sanity to the man possessed;
- Restores life to Jairus' daughter.

So Jesus is not just speaking a word for Jairus; it is a word for all of us who find ourselves beset by the chaos and absurdity of life. "Don't be afraid," he says to us, "only believe."

- Believe that what we see is not all there is.
- Believe that something else, someone else, is at work in this world.

Does this mean that our prayers will be answered and we will always get what we want? Of course not. But it does mean that we are not alone on this earth, that God gives us strength for the day, and that we can have peace in the middle of the storm that defies anything the world knows.

Maybe the best thing we can hope for in times of chaos is that God will restore us to our best selves – people of faith, people who can endure and even overcome all that comes our way.

But the lessons for today are not given only to console and strengthen us; they also call us to ministry; because the grace that comes to us always comes to us on the way to someone else. When we weather our own storms, we will find that we have changed, that we have become ministers.

That is a good word for us these days at Trinity. Because we do not have a Rector, we might be tempted to think of this season as one of waiting; and it is, of course. But we don't have the luxury of sitting back and doing nothing; the need in this community does not stop simply because Father Bob has retired. All of are called, day in and day out, to be God's person in Danville, KY, and the world.

Garrison Keillor says that when he went to high school because he lived in the country he rode the bus. On the very first day of school the principal gave every one who rode the bus a little slip of paper with the name and address of what they called their "storm home." So if a blizzard rolled through during a school day and the children could not get home, there were homes close to the school where the students could go to wait out the storm.

Keillor's storm home was with Mr. and Mrs. Krueger. Sometimes he would walk down the street and stop in front of the Krueger's little green house and say, "Well, there's my storm home. If it gets too bad, those people will take me in."

But he never went there. During his time in high school the only blizzards that came through were convenient blizzards that hit on weekends or at night. But he says he often dreamed about that little green house and the people who lived there. It became a large part of his imagination, because he knew that blizzards are not the only thing that teenagers – or adults – have to contend with. We all need places to go. If it gets too bad, we need people like the Kruegers.

If it gets too bad, we need to be people like the Kruegers. Amen.

Faithful Thomas
John 20:19-31

The Gospel of Thomas is a very early Christian writing, alleging to be written by Thomas, the Apostle. But it was written much too late, and was never included in the Bible. But Thomas has always been easy to dismiss, always known as "Doubting Thomas," as though one moment in time thoroughly defined this apostle.

Today I want to speak a word for you, a word about Thomas and his doubt, and also his faith... Without a doubt Thomas doubted that Jesus had been raised from the dead. But he was not at all the only person in the four gospels who doubted that Jesus had been raised. In fact, doubt is everywhere. It is with us here today.

The Bible reveals that even Jesus struggled with doubt:

- In the garden he prayed three times for the cup of death to be removed, but ultimately submitted to God's will.
- On the cross he prayed, "My God, my God, why hast thou forsaken me?"

Doubt is a constant theme in the stories of the resurrection:

- Matthew 28:17, when they saw Jesus (after the resurrection) they believed, but some doubted.
- Mark 16, they would not believe that Mary had seen the risen Lord.

- Luke 24, the stories of Jesus' resurrection seemed to the disciples like an idle tale.

So why preach a sermon on doubt? We need to hear this today because some Christians think that faith in God, real faith, excludes all doubt. That simply is not true. Faith is not certainty, but believing because of the uncertainty. Genuine faith swims in a sea of a thousand doubts.

The wonderful movie, *The Cinderella Man*, is the true story of Jim Braddock. It starts George Clooney and Renee Zellweger. It is the story of a boxer and his family during the Great Depression. Braddock, through a combination of injury and bad luck, has lost everything. He struggles to keep the utilities turned on in the little apartment where he lives with his wife and three small children. They are always cold and hungry, and illness hounds the children.

After a day of trying to find some kind of work, without success, Braddock returned home. It was cold, and he could hear his children coughing in their sleep. His wife served up what little food they had, and began to pray, "Lord we are grateful..." She looked up to see her husband just sitting there. "Aren't you going to pray with me," she asked? And he said, "I'm all prayed out."

I first began to experience doubt about my faith when I went off to Berea College. My doubts were not the result of science classes about evolution or the fact that the world is millions of years old. No, it was when I attended religion classes that employed the very best and thorough methods of biblical study available at that time. I struggled when I discovered that other people had their own creation stories and flood stories, because I wanted the Bible to be unique.

I had heated conversations with the Baptist director of campus ministry, Paul Larson, because I could not bring myself to abandon the beliefs of my childhood. Paul called me to a broader faith, and to this day he remains my friend.

The other day I had a conversation with one of you in which I commented, "It is not important that we come up with the right answers. It is, however, vitally important that we ask the right questions."

These days I am not troubled about my doubts, because I see them as leading me forward to a more open and genuine faith. I realized years ago that if Jesus is the Truth, then our pursuit of truth will lead us towards God, not away from God.

The good news is, that we are saved by being in a loving relationship with God through Jesus Christ.

- We don't have to be right about everything;
- We don't have to believe without a doubt. No.

All that is needed is that we accept that God accepts us. The rest is just our growing into God's love. Amen.